You're Not the Boss of Me!
A Guide to Leadership
Development

Kristine D. Jones-Pasley, PhD

Copyright Information

You're Not the Boss of Me!
A Guide to Leadership Development

"Jesus said to him, 'If you can believe, all things are possible to him who believes.'" (Mark 9:23)

This is dedicated to my Georgie, who believes I can do anything.

Table of Contents

You're Not the Boss of Me!

CHAPTER ONE
Who Are You?

I will tell you from the start, this is not your normal, warm and fuzzy leadership book. This is not a Jack Welch management and leadership text. My hope is that this book will make you think about leadership in general and your leadership style specifically.

Leadership is similar to porn; you can't define it, but you know it when you see it. Have you thought about the fact that there are many definitions of leadership? No, two writers seem to provide the same definition.

Let's look at the basic definition of leadership. Merriam-Webster.com (2017) defines leadership *(noun)* as "a position as leader of a group, organization, etc.; the time when a person holds the position of leader; the power or ability to lead other people." Let's be honest, for a layperson, this definition is okay. However, for those of us in the business of leadership, the definition tells us absolutely nothing.

What is leadership? What do the academic researchers have to say? You will find in academia that there is no one agreed upon definition of leadership. Like laypeople, academics tend to focus on traits and behaviors that support leadership theories. Some of the more popular characteristics (traits) and behaviors to describe leaders are confident, assertive, visionary, charismatic and the list goes on and on. When you think about it, these can describe just about anyone on any given day. Put someone in the right situation and these characteristics or behaviors may show up.

Trying to define leadership is difficult. There are many variables to consider and analyze. However, I will give you my thoughts on leadership. I believe that leadership is founded in a relationship...an influential relationship. Relationships are about more than family. Relationships are about connections. How are you connected to another person? How can you use your influence to get that person to do something? My definition: *Leadership is using an influence in a relationship to get an individual(s) (followers, employees, team members) to accomplish a goal or objective.* Some definitions of leadership describe the goal or objective as "shared." I left this term out of my definition as sometimes the goal or objective is not immediately seen as shared. As a leader, you may need to use your influence to get the individuals (followers, employees, team members) to see that it is a "shared" goal or objective.

So, as a person in a leadership position or someone who considers himself or herself a leader, how would you define leadership? Do you look at the traits and behaviors of a person; or do you determine leadership status by a position held?

Leader vs Boss

I am sure you are wondering why the title of the book is "You're Not the Boss of Me!" I will put it out there, I cannot stand the term "boss." It grates my soul when I hear someone refer to another as their boss or they call someone boss. I cannot stand it. Let's go back to the dictionary and define boss. Merriam-Webster (2017) states a boss *(noun)* is "a person who exercises control or authority; specifically, one who directs or supervises workers; a politician, who controls votes in a party organization or dictates appointments or legislative measures." In urban vernacular boss (or bawse) has a similar connotation. It still means someone who is in charge and has a strong personality.

I do not know about you, but I do not want to be referred to as someone's boss. Boss is not a term of endearment and as a leader, it is not a title that you should want. You are probably saying "well, it is not that big a deal," it should be if you want to be a positive, effective, and respected leader. Remember, children do not go around saying "you are not the manager/supervisor/leader of me;" they say "you are not the boss of me!"

If being a boss is what you want to be, then go for it; but you need to realize you cannot "rule" with an iron fist and a boss-like attitude for long and build a lasting and respectful relationship with your employees. As we discussed before, leadership is founded in a relationship. Being a boss, you have formed a relationship; usually, it is a relationship built on fear or intimidation. Do you want your employees fearing you or do you want them to listen to you and get the job done knowing that there is a feeling of mutual respect?

You are probably saying, "well, I can't be a pushover." When did being kind and respectful to others equate to being a pushover? You hired adults for a specific position; treat them as the professionals they are. Would you appreciate someone speaking to you the way you speak to others? If the answer is no, you need to re-evaluate and make some changes.

Being a leader is about connection. Some of the best leaders were able to connect with people. It is up to you if you want that connection to be positive or negative. Yes, for a short time you can get things done with a negative connection; however, if you want to see growth in your employees, you are going to have to incorporate positivity.

Are You a Leader or a Person in a Leadership Position?

In my research, I have found many different articles trying to define leadership. Some articles have gone so far as to just matter-of-factly state that leadership is anyone in a management, supervisory, or "boss" position.

There goes that word "boss." Why are leader and boss used interchangeably? In your leadership position, do you feel like a "boss" or a member of the team that you happen to lead? My hope is that you said you feel like a member of the team. As a leader, if you do not feel like a member of the team that may be your #1 problem with leading your team.

There is a big difference between being a leader and being a person in a leadership position. Remember, in order to lead, you must have someone to lead. If your team does not come to you and goes to another person on the team for advice and help, guess what? You are a person in a leadership position and the person that your team depends on is the leader.

Now, you may be saying that "maybe my team doesn't want to bother me with certain details." You may have a point; however, if team members do not feel comfortable coming to you, that is a problem. Have you stated, "do not come to me with minor issues?" Does your team need to jump through hoops before they can speak with you?

If this information sounds familiar, you are not acting like a leader. You are acting like the great and powerful Oz, you know the mystical character from the movie, the Wizard of Oz. You do not want to be bothered with what is happening in the team. Even if you have team leads to handle certain things, every team member should be comfortable with coming to you should an issue arise. There is nothing worse than human resources (HR) contacting you stating that a problem has been brought to their attention and you had no idea something was wrong.

Being a great leader is a balancing act. Yes, you want to be open and approachable, but you also need to ensure that you do not take on too much. How do you do this? Check in with the team. You should meet with your team at least once per week for a short 10-15-minute check in. It doesn't have to be long and drawn out, just let them see your face and hear your voice.

If you have team leads, meet with them as a group for a short 10-15-minute check in. Ask what is going on with the team. Are there any issues that you should be made aware of? Now, unless the team lead states that they need you to take over, just take all that they say as information. File it away should something happen and you are asked about the situation. A key to being a successful leader is knowing when to let your team handle their business like the professionals that they are.

Effective vs Good (Positive)

Answer this question: are you an effective leader or a good (positive) leader? You are asking yourself what is the difference. Look at it this way, think about some of the most polarizing leaders of yesterday and today (for example: Fidel Castro, Jim Jones, Saddam Hussein, etc.), although many of them were effective leaders; would you classify them as good (positive) leaders? If you are a good leader;

effectiveness is already there. Many individuals think that in order to be effective, kindness has to go out the window. That is not true. Remember, leadership is a relationship. Who does not want to be in a relationship with kindness and respect? How long do you think it will take before people get tired of following someone who is mean and ugly to them? The saying "do not take my kindness for weakness" is a true statement. No one is saying that you have to be a speed bump; however, you must learn to balance out sternness and kindness. An effective leader will "get the job done" but at what cost?

An effective leader is motivating but what is behind that motivation? Adolf Hitler was motivating; however, he motivated and pandered to people's fears and hate. The ability to motivate is a dangerous thing. You could motivate someone into doing something that is far outside their character and could destroy them. A good leader will balance effectiveness and motivation by ensuring how they motivate people draws out the positive. Again, do not confuse effectiveness with being good (positive).

Well, you may be saying, "good" is too simple a word to describe leadership. What happened to being good? Why have we decided that in order to be an effective leader, brow-beating and down talk is the way to motivate people into doing what we want when we want. A good effective leader will motivate people into doing what is needed even if they do not understand how all the pieces fit together. A boss will use the motivation of "do it because I said so and this is my vision." A good effective leader will have people buying into the vision and will want to do it because it is "our vision."

Leadership Examples (Bad vs Good)

One of the worst supervisors I had was at my first job out of college as an assistant branch manager at a bank. The bank that I worked for had a management trainee program that all new managers and assistant managers worked through. During this training, we were required to rotate through various departments and bank branches. My first branch rotation was at Jane's branch. I would describe her as a supervisor, but we could call her a negative effective leader. Technically, she was not my supervisor, but she was a senior branch manager and vice president (do not ask why she had the title of VP and senior branch manager, I have no idea).

Jane had a reputation of being tough and I was told she was the best to learn from if I wanted a great career at the bank. I was interested in seeing what she was all about. She ruled her branch with an iron fist. All members of her team had great respect *(now that I think about it, I have to wonder if it was more fear than traditional respect)* for her position and would tiptoe around her when she was in a "mood." I did learn a lot from her, the biggest lesson being what not to do in a leadership position.

Everyone was afraid of this woman. The vice president, who was the supervisor for the trainees, cowed to her. It had gotten so bad with her I had called him and asked to be transferred.

What I did not know was that he called and told her what I said! This was an awkward situation, but the funny thing was she had respect for me because I was not going to take her junk. *(Jane actually told me he told her what I said!)*

The rotation through her branch was an odd time, but I learned a lot about myself and my skills of observation increased. I started paying attention to the members of her team. I saw how her team interacted with each other, her, and her assistant branch manager. I think this started my road to researching leadership. I wanted to understand why people would tolerate being yelled at, cursed at, etc., by a supervisor and how this motivated *(or not)* them to complete their tasks. I would describe this woman as a "boss."

She told you to jump and you better say how high!

One of the best leaders I had was when I worked as a technical trainer. Sam allowed his team members the freedom to get the job done in a manner that was efficient to them. I spoke with Sam about the process of creating training and how I worked better at home. I did not have the distractions at home that I had at work. *(At the time, I was single and I could shut out the world and create the training needed.)* I asked Sam if I could work from home. Now, this was before telecommuting became a big thing. I was also a government contractor and as such, we needed to have our face at the customer site.

Sam looked at me and said "okay." He did not question me; he did not threaten me with what would happen if I did not get my training completed. I went home and created the three-day training assignment that I had. The next day, I came in and typed it up *(did I mention that I was old school and handwrote the entire training course?)* and submitted it. Sam came over and spoke about how good a job I had done on the training.

Within 30-days or so, I was tasked to be the lead trainer for a major system to be rolled out worldwide. There was a lot of visibility regarding this new system and processes involved in using the system. Looking back, I was shocked that I was selected to be the lead trainer as I was the new kid on the block and there were more senior trainers available. However, Sam saw something in me and he tasked me, with being the lead trainer.

When it was time to sit down and create the training, I went to Sam again and asked if I could work from home and create the training. Again, Sam said yes. He had faith in me to do what I needed to do and get the job done.

Although the system had high visibility, Sam trusted me as the lead trainer to attend meetings and work with the customer directly. If I had problems or questions, I would go to Sam and he would provide advice and ask me about my comfort level in handling the situation. You see, if needed, Sam would step in and help, but he motivated me into trusting myself and my abilities to get the job done without him having to step in.

Sam was a good and effective leader. He knew how to motivate without making people feel like he was taking over or without having to make threats. He understood that he hired people for a job and that he had to trust them to do the job they were hired for.

Sam also protected and supported his people. When questions came up regarding why I had to work from home, Sam simply stated, "that is Kris' process for creating excellent training." Even his supervisor, questioned him regarding my working from home and he gave her the same simple response. *(Side note: when I left the company, I received a certificate and glowing letter from our customer regarding the training and my leadership during the rollout of the system.)*

Being a good effective leader means you need to trust your own decisions and the people you work with. If you are questioned, fall back on your decision(s) made. Be confident in your leadership role.

Activity - What is Leadership to You?

1. How do you define leadership?

2. What are three leadership characteristics or behaviors you feel that every good leader should possess? Do you feel that you have these characteristics or behaviors? (If you said no, determine how you can develop them.)

3. How do you view the term "boss"?

4. Which leader in your career greatly influenced your leadership style? Why? (Give an example of a negative effective leader and a positive effective (good) leader.)

5. How would your team describe your leadership skills? What are your strengths? What are your weaknesses?

CHAPTER TWO
What Does a Leader Look Like?

For many who are new leaders, they do not know their leadership identity (to tell the truth, there are many "experienced" leaders who do not know their leadership identity). New leaders tend to read books, look to individuals on television, around the office, and in their families for help in forming a leadership identity. They may try to emulate the personality trait and characteristics of the people they see and read about. That is not what you want to do as you can only fake it for so long before your true personality comes out. **Be yourself from day one.**

Now, there is a caveat with being yourself, you want to be your professional, appropriate self in the workplace. No one is saying that you need to be fake, but you need to know when to dial it back. For example, if you are a "straight shooter," there is a time and place for that. Not everyone will appreciate your lack of tact, you may need to gauge your wording so that you do not sound harsh. You can still "tell it like it is" but you need to have tact when you do it.

Another issue comes to mind in that many people do not have a self-identity in general. It seems that the new trend is to "find yourself." Hopefully, as a leader, you already know who you are as a person and have a solid foundation. Not knowing who you are and not being comfortable with who you are can lead to moral and ethical challenges in the workplace (and in your personal life). If you do not know who you are, how do you expect anyone else to know and want to respect you?

"I Want Everyone to Like Me"...No You Don't

For some leaders, they associate being liked with being a good leader. Guess what? Not everyone is going to like you, but you do want people to respect you and your decisions. I am not sure when the "I want to be liked by everyone" movement happened, but it needs to end. In the workplace, everyone should get along, have fun, and get the job done. Stop trying to be everyone's friend. Now, this is not to say you should not be friendly, but remember, there is a difference between being friendly and being someone's friend.

How Do I Read People?

This is a difficult question to answer. As a leader, you need to be able to read people through body language and tone. This is not to say you are going to be a walking lie detector like the television show Lie to Me. It does mean that you need to be able to focus on others and garner what is going on by looking at body language and tone.

The one thing I dislike is looking people in the eyes when they speak. I tend to zone out and I do not hear a word they say. A body language "expert" would think that I am hiding something, the truth is I get mesmerized and I do not pay attention to what they are saying. Don't get me wrong, when I speak to people I look at them, I just do not look them in their eyes because quite frankly (outside of being mesmerized) it creeps me out. I look at people so that they know I am speaking to them, but I am not staring them down. If you have little quirks, let people know up front so that they are not offended.

Reading people is about paying attention. Believe me, just because I may not be looking you in the eyes, doesn't mean I am not paying attention to you. Remember, I am looking at you. I may notice how you tap your hands on the armchair when you have something important to tell me. I will notice how you run your hands down your pants when you have something to tell me that I may not be happy about. Be careful in assuming that people are not listening to you just because they may not give you all the social cues you are looking for. What are your quirks?

Social Media

Social media is a touchy subject for many. Millennials live for documenting every aspect of their lives. The majority of baby boomers think social media is the devil. As a leader, you need to keep your social media presence professional. I would even recommend having separate social media accounts, one for business associates and an account for family and close friends. The VP of Logistics does not need to see you in your bathing suit on the beach in Jamaica.

For me, my Facebook account is for family and close friends. I do not have current co-workers on my Facebook account and never business associates. If I become close with a co-worker and it leads to friendship, I do not friend them on Facebook until one of us leaves the company. That is a quirk that I have regarding my social media. I had a Facebook account where my students could reach me; however, I shut that down and now, my students can reach me via LinkedIn.

You want to be very careful in who you "friend" on the various social media platforms and what you say on the various social media platforms. People constantly say they have freedom of speech...you do, but also recognize those freedoms come with consequences should you say something that is offensive.

Encourage your team to be careful with social media. I will never forget, a woman in the office was

Facebook "friends" with several co-workers in the office. The woman called in sick but on Facebook, announced she was out and about having fun. Guess what? One of her "friends" leaked that she was not sick but just didn't want to come to work and was out having fun. How do you think that went over?

Folks, the whole world does not need to know what you are doing every minute of the day. Now, the woman probably wanted to take a mental health break to go and have some fun; there is nothing wrong with that. The problem came in when she decided to post what she was doing on Facebook for everyone to see. **Keep private things private**.

Activity – What is it about you?

1. What are your quirks? What do you do that may be out of the social norms when you communicate with people?

2. How often do you feel the need to have everyone like you? Why? If you do not feel the need to have everyone like you, how did you get to this stage in your life? Have you always been like that or did something happen to make you feel that way?

3. What are your top two questions regarding leadership? Where have you looked to help answer the questions?

4. What social media platforms do you
   have? Do you have employees (co-
   workers) on your social media?
   Why?

Activity – While you were on vacation...

You just get back from vacation and there is a storm of controversy. Your team lead, whom you left in charge while you were on your one-week vacation, posted information regarding the disciplinary action of a team member on Facebook and it got back to the team member. The disciplined team member is calling for the team lead to be fired for leaking sensitive information.

Here are the facts:

1. The team lead did not mention any names. He stated "Had to write a guy up for looking at porn on his work computer. What is

wrong with him? People have no shame."

2. The team member who was disciplined heard about the posting through a mutual associate.

3. The entire team is up in arms because they want to know who the "sicko" is that was looking at porn at work. (You do not know who told the team.)

What do you do?

1. What is the internet policy at your office? (If you do not know off the top of your head, stop now and go find out.)

2. Who do you speak with first? The team lead or the team member written up for watching porn?

3. Do you investigate who told the team? Why? Why not?

4. How do you address the team regarding the controversy?

Create a detailed plan of action.

CHAPTER THREE
Communication

Communication is one of the easiest ways to create chaos. (I think I should trademark that saying.) If you search for the types of communication, you will find information ranging from three to six types of communication. I stand on three types of communication: verbal, written, and non-verbal. Now, an argument can be made for a number of "sub-types;" however, this is not my academic classroom and honestly, the three I stated are what I call "the biggies." *(Frankly, all communication should fall within one of these three types.)*

Verbal communication is just that, communication that is spoken.

This type of communication can be conducted face-to-face, via telephone, Skype, etc.

Written communication is printed information. This includes emails, blogs, company policies, letters, etc.

Non-verbal communication is the "expression on your face." Non-verbal communication can be "seen" as social cues or body language. I placed seen in quotes as non-verbal communication can cover written communication also, the "tone" of your email.

As a leader, you want your communication style to be free of causing chaos. Think for a minute on how you communicate with your team. Is the majority of the communication chaos free? Do you often get follow-up questions on what you have said or emailed? How is your body language when you speak to the team? Do you cross your arms in front of you? Do you look around when someone is speaking to you? Is your communication conducted mostly through email?

Verbal Communication

When thinking of communication chaos, verbal communication is right at the top. How many times have you had someone misunderstand what you stated? How many times have you spoken before your brain fully finished processing what should have been spoken? Here are my top three tips for effective verbal communication:

1. **THINK** before you speak. Seriously, how many of us have said something that we wished we could literally grab the words out of the air after

they were spoken? Pause before speaking. If you need time to gather your thoughts, tell the person to give you a minute so that you formulate an appropriate response.

2. Speak clearly and concisely. Do not speak to someone with a mouth full of gum or candy. You want to speak clearly so that you are heard. Do not ramble as you speak. If you need to have a bullet list of speaking topics for yourself, do it. You want your message to come out clearly and succinctly.

3. Be confident. Be confident, not arrogant. Watch your body language. Those non-verbal cues such as slouching, crossing your arms in front of you, etc. (We will discuss this further down in the chapter). If you think before you speak, and you

speak clearly and concisely, this will bring about confidence.

Written Communication

You would assume that written communication would help alleviate chaos. WRONG. Written communication can bring about just as much chaos as verbal (think about Twitter and Facebook and the drama that can bring). In business, email is the #1 source used for written communication. For many leaders/managers/supervisors, email is their go-to style of communication. Is it yours?

If you stated that the majority of your communication is conducted through email, identify why you use email as the major source of communication. If you lead a virtual team, then this is understandable. However, if your team is sitting outside your office door or sitting in the cubicles surrounding you, take a moment and analyze why you do not get up and go speak with them face-to-face.

Now, let me pause here for a moment. Some of you may be up in arms regarding my questions and that is okay. However, you should ask yourself, why are you up in arms regarding communication? Has a team member asked why you are sending an email and they sit next to you?

I am not against email. Email has saved my bacon many times. However, what is wrong with getting up from your desk and speaking to someone and then following up the conversation with an email? You still have the conversation on record, but you can also get immediate feedback on questions and such without a lot of back and forth in a long email string.

When using email, follow these tips:

1. When composing an email, type it up in Word (or some other word processing software). This helps with 1. You won't accidentally send a message that is still a work in progress and 2. You can wordsmith the heck out of the message before sending it.

2. Outline what you want to say. How can you tell someone something if you don't organize the information? This is especially important for emails that involve directions.

3. Use spell and grammar check. There is nothing more distracting than

reading an email with spelling and grammar issues.

4. Send the email at the right time. Do not send a detailed instruction filled email five minutes before the team member(s) is set to leave for the day. Send it in the morning or wait 30 minutes after they have left for the day. This way they have the message first thing in the morning. If you must send it at the end of the day, the first line after the greeting should be something like "This can wait until tomorrow. I just wanted to get the information to you so that you would see it first thing in the morning."

5. End the email by encouraging the person (people) to contact you if there are any questions or concerns. It is amazing how many people will

send out a detailed email and then not state they are available for questions. When you do not do this, it makes the receiver(s) of the email hesitant to contact you when there are issues. Note, you may end up making the message sound like a directive that must be done to the letter with no questions asked.

Honestly, we need to get back to utilizing more verbal communication in our teams. Often, we focus on written communication as a way to interact with the team. Sometimes, it is just best to get up and go speak with the team.

Non-verbal Communication

How is your body language? Do you have a poker face or does your face speak volumes? I will be the first to admit, my face will tell everything. I have to be very aware of my body language when I am out in public. When I am teaching/training, I have my "professional" shield on and I am cognizant of my body language. In social settings, I think I relax too much and forget that I need to be more aware. Think about it for a moment, are you able to separate your professional "face/body" from your personal "face/body?"

One of the most closed off stances you can have when speaking to someone is crossing your arms. If you do not want people to approach you, stand with your arms crossed. You look uninviting and you are saying to everyone, "do not approach me." I invite you to search "body language where to place hands" on the Internet. There are a list of gestures and such that you may be doing that are distracting to the message you are trying to convey.

Active Listening

The topic of active listening is a hot one. I wanted to break it out of the verbal or some will place it under non-verbal category. I wanted the topic to have a section as it is such an important one and I did not want it to get lost in the other topics.

I have to ask, when people speak, are you listening to respond or are you listening to understand? This is one of the oldest questions regarding active listening. Many times, people are not listening but waiting for an opportunity to make their own point. As a leader, you **<u>must</u>** ensure that you are actively listening to people.

Active listening is not just about your ears, it is also about your body language. You want to ensure that you are showing interest, look at the speaker, do not fold your arms while they are speaking, and stay relaxed but focused. While the person is speaking, do not interrupt, let him or her finish. In the conversation, you should be able to tell if they are asking for an opinion/help or just needing someone to listen to them. If you are unsure if they are asking for your opinion/help, you can ask them, "are you asking me for something or just need a listening ear?" Remember, everyone who comes to you may not need you to solve anything, they just may need to bounce an idea aloud.

When it is time to respond, think about the verbal tips discussed above. It is okay to take a moment and pause before responding. There is no shame in telling someone you will get back with them if you are unable to make a quick decision. You want the person to know that you heard them, you are processing what they said, and that you are gathering your thoughts to provide an appropriate response. Remember, THINK before you speak.

Will You Listen to Me...Please?!

Individuals in leadership positions tend to think that everyone should listen to them about everything. Guess what? Many times, you sound like the adults on the Peanuts cartoons. Just because you may be in a leadership position does not mean you have the oratory skills of Dr. Martin Luther King, Jr.

One area of frustration for many leaders is ensuring that people take them seriously when they speak. Here are six ways to get people to take you seriously. Note: This is not an all-inclusive list, but it is a good start.

1. Active listening. We just spoke about this, allow others to speak and to ensure that you are in the moment and listening. Remember, listen for understanding not for when you can jump in with your opinion.

2. Watch your tone. When speaking, you do not want to come off condescending. You want to speak with confidence not arrogance.

3. Make statements not questions. Have you noticed when you get nervous speaking to someone (or a group of people) you end sentences

as questions instead of statements? You want people to listen to you, think about what you are saying and process it. You do not want people wondering about your knowledge on the subject/topic.

4. Stay knowledgeable. You should know about new technologies, processes, etc., related to your industry. Get a subscription to a journal in your industry, read the paper (either hard copy or soft copy), join an association, etc. Stay in the know.

5. Be confident. This is not only about how you speak, but how you present yourself, do not mutter, speak clearly. Do not put someone else down to make yourself look better that is not confidence it is pettiness.

Again, be confident, but not arrogant.

6. Dress the part. Now, I know that the dress code for many businesses is much more casual than it used to be but this does not mean you get to wear your "It is 5 o'clock Somewhere" t-shirt and your jeans with holes in the knees. You can still look professional in a pair of nice jeans and a shirt. The key is to look clean and neat.

Let's pause here for a moment and speak about piercings and tattoos. For a certain generation, these two areas are a strict no-no; however, nowadays it may be difficult to find a millennial (or many people for that matter) that does not have a few or more of each. If you have piercings and tattoos, you know what is appropriate for your work environment and what is not. **Use common sense when you are dressing each day.**

7. Give credit where credit is due. It is important to know your team. This means not only the team members that like to be seen and heard but those that are quite contributors. No matter how hard it may be to give credit, you must do so as it shows that you respect your team members and their contributions. Take a moment and think about a time when you were not given credit. How did that make you feel? Do you want others to feel that way?

It is not always easy to get people to listen to every word you speak. You have to remember, that sometimes there are individuals who will not listen to you no matter what you say or how you say it. Confidence is one of the main keys in being a good leader. You cannot be wishy-washy and doubting who you are and what you are.

Activity - Communication

1. Describe the communication process within your team.

2. Who is the one person on the team (outside of you) that the majority of the team depends on? What is your relationship like with that person? (Does the person intimidate you?)

3. How would your team describe your communication skills? What are your strengths? What are your weaknesses?

4. How can you encourage communication within your team? List two specific action items.

Activity – What did they say?

Even while watching television or listening to our favorite music, we can tune out and filter information. For this exercise, watch the first 10 minutes of a television show and afterward respond to the following:

1. What is the name of the television show?

2. What is the day of the week and time the show comes on?

3. What is the name of the episode?

4. Who is the first character to speak?

5. What is the first word they say?

6. Summarize the first 10 minutes of the episode.

7. How many characters speak during the first 10 minutes?

8. What are the commercials?

9. Who is the last character to speak?

10. What is the last word spoken?

How hard was it to pay attention?

Did you find yourself wondering while watching and listening?

CHAPTER FOUR
Motivation

One of the areas that most leadership (management) teams are looking for help is motivation. "How can we motivate our employees?" "How can we maintain motivation?" Here is a tip...motivation is rooted in appreciation. Do you appreciate your team (employees)? Now, you may be saying, "they get a salary, that should be good enough." Guess what...it is not good enough. People want to know what they are doing is appreciated.

Let's get to the basics, motivation is about personal gain. "What's in it for me?" Motivating people can be a challenging concept. Sometimes it is as easy as buying pizza once a month to show appreciation and sometimes it is all about the money. Early in my career, I had a saying "keep the accolades, give me the money." In my younger days, I was motivated by money. I wanted bonuses and salary increases. You could keep the awards and kudos.

You will have to determine what motivates your team. (Don't forget about your motivation also. We will discuss that later.) Sometimes your employees will tell you point blank what motivates them and what they are looking for to maintain motivation. In many cases, you will have to ask about their goals and motivation.

When you ask, be sincere in wanting to know. Speaking with and getting to know your team is another brick in the foundation of the relationship that you are building with them. You may even want your team to fill out a self-assessment to help them and you determine their motivating factors. There are TONS of self-assessments online, go out and conduct a search to find one that isn't long and tedious but fun to fill out.

You have to think about this, how can you ask someone to give 100% if you do not appreciate what they do, let alone if they go above and beyond their "duties?" Even if they are "just doing their job," a simple "thank you" can go a long way.

When I was an assistant branch manager at a bank years ago, I constantly told my staff thank you and one my Customer Service Representatives (CSRs) told me, "Kristine, you can thank a person to death." I just laughed. It is instinctual for me to say thank you. I want people to understand that I appreciate what they are doing, no matter how large or small.

So, how can you motivate your employees? Learn to appreciate what they do for the team and the company. Do not just wait until the yearly review to provide praise, you should be doing this often. What many companies fail to realize is that when employees feel appreciated, they build loyalty to the organization. (Loyalty is another area that many companies are wondering how to instill in their employees.) During your weekly meetings, give kudos. You can do this in an email also.

Note: In your company Internet, there should be an area for kudos. If this is not currently incorporated, speak to someone (or if you have the authority) to get it done immediately. You can set it up where employees can send an email and either HR or IT posts the information on the site. You will be surprised how good people feel when they realize they have received a kudos.

Self-Motivation

I wanted to take a moment and look at self-motivation. What motivates you as a leader? Why do you want to be a leader? What do you like about being a leader? *(Note: If your response is, "I like telling people what to do," you are in trouble.)* What do you find most challenging about being a leader? How do you re-center yourself after a difficult or challenging decision is made or implemented?

Although you want to ensure that your team is motivated, you have to ensure that you too are on the motivated train. If you find that leadership is becoming overwhelming, tedious, etc., speak to a mentor immediately. You do not want your lack of motivation to bleed over into the team. Maybe the only thing you need to rejuvenate yourself is a vacation. When was your last vacation? How are you taking care of yourself?

Constructive Criticism (Feedback)

One of my favorite scripture passages is "Death and life are in the power of the tongue, and those who love it will eat its fruit" (Proverbs 18:21). This statement is so powerful. You must understand that what you say has power...end of story. What you say to people can plant a seed and take root. As a leader, you want to plant powerful positive seeds in everyone you meet. You never know what one small word can do for someone, so be very careful in what you say and how you say it.

Constructive criticism (also known as constructive feedback) is an area of leadership that can make people uncomfortable. Providing feedback that may not be positive can be daunting, but it must be done sometimes. How you provide feedback is just as important as what you say. **NEVER** give constructive criticism in a public forum. You do not want to embarrass someone in front of their peers. That can backfire on you. You want to provide feedback in a one-on-one setting. One-on-one can be face-to-face, Skype, telephone, email, etc. You want it so that only the person and you are involved.

One of the hardest pieces of feedback to give is on someone's idea. You want your team members to come to you with ideas; however, sometimes the idea does not have a solid foundation. One way to get people to see that the idea has challenges is to get them to conduct a deep dive. Ask them to conduct an analysis of their idea, give them a list of questions to address. You will be surprised at how they will then find some of the issues on their own. Now, if they do not find the challenges you saw, you will have to sit them down and discuss where you found issues. If you have to go this route, have notes and be specific. Do not associate the issues with the team member as a person but focus on the idea. You can state, "this area of the recommendation needs to look at..." You are taking the focus off the person and putting it on the idea. Remember, you want them to recognize it is the idea that has challenges, not him or her personally.

Conflict Resolution

I decided to separate conflict resolution from constructive criticism as I feel the two topics are different. Constructive criticism is a focus on work performance/ideas and how to improve on certain areas. Conflict resolution...there is a behavioral issue that needs to be addressed.

As a leader, your greatest wish is for everyone to get along. You hope that when issues arise, everyone can behave as adults and work out the situation. Let me stop you right there. Unfortunately, in the work environment responsible adults can become 16 or 17-year-old juniors in high school. When I think back on some of the immature issues that happened in the various offices I worked in, I cringe. I have to wonder if the people realized they were acting like children.

My Master's degree is in Human Resources Development; I admit, I did not want to deal with employee relations. I know me, and if someone came to me talking about another employee did not like them, my first response would be "is that going to affect your meeting the deadline?" I freely admit I have a low tolerance for juvenile behavior. I did not deal well with gossip and pettiness in high school and I do not deal with it well in a business environment.

You must ensure that you stop petty, immature, unprofessional behavior in its tracks. As a leader, you need to show a high level of maturity, no matter how hard it may be (trust me, there will be times where it will be hard to bite your tongue). When things happen and the issues are brought to your attention, you need to investigate immediately. Do not wait as you do not want the situation to get out of control.

When in doubt on how to handle a situation, contact HR. They will help you in making sure you are following company policies and procedures along with laws, rules, and regulations. Like constructive criticism, you do not want to reprimand someone in a group setting. It should be behind closed doors and if possible have an HR representative there to help facilitate if need be. You may read plenty of articles and books on how to speak to someone regarding a reprimand, I will tell you the truth, it is hard and can be very uncomfortable. Do not be surprised if afterwards, you are upset also. My number one tip, speak to HR and ask them how to handle this area. Every situation is different, speaking to Jim about coming to work late every morning is totally different from speaking to Jill about inappropriate and offensive jokes.

Remember, being a leader does not mean you have to know everything or handle all things on your own. A good leader knows when to bring in reinforcements.

Activity – What is going on with your team?

You have a team of 33. The teams are broken into three teams of 11 members (Team A, Team B, and Team C) with a single team lead. Each Wednesday morning at 10:00 AM, you have a team meeting with the entire group. At 10:30 AM, you have a meeting with the team leads. This Wednesday morning, team leader B comes to you at 9:45 AM to tell you that he saw, team leader A being sexually harassed by one of her male team members. Team leader B goes on to state that the team member doing the harassing is the one he requested to be moved to team A because the team member was harassing women on team B. You were never made aware of why the transfer was being made, you knew that the team member worked well with the customer and made all deadlines.

What are you going to do?

1. Provide details of your investigative process to determine what is going on and how to handle the situation?

    a. Should team leader B be reprimanded for not disclosing why the team member was being moved? Why or why not?

    b. How will you confront the team member doing the harassing?

    c. How will you approach leader A regarding the information from leader B?

2. What is your company policy on sexual harassment?

3. Who is your HR representative?

If you are unable to answer questions 2 and 3 off the top of your head, locate that information immediately.

Activity – Who did what?

You have a major deadline upcoming and it looks like you all will not make it. Kelly, the quiet engineer, has an idea on how to cut time and has shared this information with her team leader, Cory. Cory presents the idea to you, but has not mentioned that the idea came from Kelly. You agree with the idea and it is implemented. You all make the deadline.

You want to reward the team and Cory specifically. You host a pizza party for the team and award Cory with a $100 cash reward for the great idea. Cory accepts the award and thanks the team.

Two weeks later, Kelly comes to you with her letter of resignation. You ask why and she explains that the idea Cory presented was hers and she is tired of Cory not giving credit for her ideas. Kelly informs you that she has several emails to prove ideas presented in the last two months were hers and not that of Cory.

1. What do you do?

2. How would you handle the issue of Cory?

3. How would you go about keeping Kelly on the team?

CHAPTER FIVE
But...But...I Am New!

We are now going to focus on newly promoted leaders. These are the people that were promoted from within the organization to a leadership position. I found that many organizations have stepped away from leadership (supervisor or management) training. This is a big issue. Why? You now have a team member that has been promoted from within but does not know how to function in a leadership (supervisor or management) position. It is wonderful that the company wants to promote from within; however, they need to ensure that those who are being promoted have the skills necessary to lead the team.

Being promoted is an exciting time. You have new responsibilities, and let's face it...the pay increase is great also. The downside of the promotion is that you know all the team secrets and now it is your responsibility to address any issues affecting the team. How do you speak to Carol about taking a smoke break every hour on the hour for 15 minutes? How do you address Nathan about his 2.5-hour lunches?

As a newly promoted leader (supervisor or manager), it is in your best interest to start strong. You do not want to seem wishy washy. One way to address the team secrets is by having a team meeting. In the meeting, you lay out your expectations and incorporate the company policies. This achieves two things. First, you can state your position in a group setting for all to hear. Many individuals are not comfortable with one-on-one conversations (ok...confrontation), so a group setting will help address that uncomfortableness. Secondly, stating the company policies lets your team know that as the leader (supervisor or manager) you will abide by and enforce company policies. Follow up the meeting with an email, that way everything is in writing. Now, you have laid the foundation for your expectations and company policies.

Company Policies and Procedures

I am sure we can all admit that as a team member, we may be only slightly familiar with the policies and procedures of our company. Be honest, have you really read the code of conduct or handbook, or did you skim it? Do you read the handbook only for something specific? As a new leader, you need to know it. Now, that is not to say you need to know it verbatim, but you should know it enough to find the information you may need for various situations. For example, you should know where to find the sexual harassment policy.

Many organizations have their policies online in the company intranet, **bookmark it**. You could even create a cheat sheet that you have on your computer that has the topic and page number and paragraph number so that you can get to the information quickly.

Human Resources (HR)

It is shocking that many employees do not know the members of their HR department. They just remember meeting Jerry on the first day to fill out paperwork and attend basic training...the end. For many employees, HR is this mystical department that processes timesheets, leave, pay, benefits, and training. Employees do not know who they are and in some cases where the department is in the building.

As a leader, you need to know who is in HR. Build a relationship with the HR team as they will be your first line of defense in keeping you and the company out of trouble.

Meetings

For many of us, meetings are a pain in the behind. There is usually no agenda, no one knows why weekly meetings are held and why they must be held on Mondays at 8:30 AM or Fridays at 3:30 PM. Do not be that leader who holds meetings just to have a meeting.

Each and every meeting that you have should have some sort of purpose. You should state the purpose in the meeting invitation.

As I mentioned earlier, you should check in with your team at least once per week for a short meeting. Again, 10-15 minutes...done. For anything that needs a detailed conversation set up a lengthy meeting at another time. One of the most irritating things about meetings is listening to a long conversation about a topic that does not affect you and what you are working on.

When setting up meetings, do not have meetings first thing Monday morning or late on Fridays. Tuesday through Thursday are the best times to have meetings. Why? On Mondays, everyone is just getting back from the weekend, they are reviewing messages and statuses from the previous week. Mondays are the time to determine what the rest of the week will look like in terms of what needs to be done first. On Fridays, everyone is trying to wind down their week and go home. Tuesdays and Wednesdays are great times for the quick 10-15-minute team meeting as everyone has determined what is taking precedent for the week, they can give a status on how the project is going. Team members will be able to say when something will be completed. Thursdays are a good time to have longer meetings because any issues and updates from earlier in the week can be addressed with better (and most cases detailed) information.

One of the most aggravating things about meetings, is back-to-back meetings. A Monday morning meeting with action items, then a Tuesday meeting asking for an update. What?! Guess what? Many of your team members are working on multiple things, sitting in meetings means that they cannot address the action items they are tasked with. Give them time to get things done so that they can provide a detailed update.

Put it in Writing

One of the best pieces of advice I ever received was "put it in writing." Follow up every meeting with an email, even if it is a short meeting on what color paper to print a manual. One good way to start the email:

Hello Jane,

Thank you for taking the time to meet with me this morning. I wanted to follow up on what we agreed regarding...

You now have a paper trail of when and what was said. If something should happen, you can now refer back to your emails and state that on such and such day you met and discussed blank. Remember, memories are short, email is forever.

For every team meeting, you want someone tasked to write action items. This should be a running list. You should have the name of the team member required to perform the action, information on the action, date action was given, due date of action and any status information.

An action item list could look like this:

#	Date	Action	Team Member	Due Date	Status
1					
2					
3					
4					
5					
6					

Open Door Policy

Every leader (supervisor, manager, team lead, etc.) wants to have an "open door" policy. Now, this can be done literally, where the door to your office is always open, figuratively where you state that you have an open-door policy, or a mixture of both. However, you decide to do it, you must create boundaries. Some of your team will respect that the open-door policy is for business and not a time to drop in every hour for chit-chat. You will find that many times this is not the case and some members of the team will take advantage hoping for a leg-up with you. You will want to ensure that you are friendly and approachable but not a doormat. Do your best to never show favorites (even if you have one and yes, we all have favorite employees) as this can cause trouble later.

A possible complication arises when you are promoted from within the team. You have established relationships with your team and some of those relationships may be outside the office. You will need to speak to those that you spend time with outside the office so that they understand that in the office, you treat everyone the same. You must also state that outside the office, you do not want to talk about work. Again...find balance. You will need to determine what is going to work best for you. If possible, you may want to have at least one level of supervision between you and your friends so that it doesn't look like you are playing favorites. I cannot stress this enough, you want to remain impartial while in the office.

The Team Busybody

Almost every team has a team busybody, in urban vernacular a "snitch." You have someone who is watching what everyone is doing and reporting to you what is going on. You need to shut that person down as it can cause drama in the team. Yes, you need to know important things like legal issues; however, you do not need to know if Joel and Johnny take 5 minutes to discuss the game last night. Who cares?!

For some in leadership positions, they like having spies to see what is going on in the workplace. That can backfire as the person (or people) doing the spying will let everyone know that they are the favorite and most likely will treat team members unprofessionally. This is how you can lose great workers and never know why. You want to treat every team member as an adult and professional. They do not need someone breathing down their necks telling them what to do every moment of the day. They were hired for a purpose, let them go about their purpose.

One of the easiest ways to shut someone down who is reporting what everyone is doing is to ask what they are doing. *"Mary, have you finished ____? I ask because it seems you have a lot of time to observe the actions of your teammates."* Once Mary finishes humming and mumming, you will not have to deal with her behavior again. You may want to then go on the floor and observe Mary and the team for yourself. Remember, always check out what is being said, do not take everything as gold. There are three sides to every story, side A, side B, and the truth. You are trying to get to the truth.

Activity – Family, can't live with them...

You have just been promoted as the team lead for your 15-member team. Jim, the lead engineer, is your brother-in-law and has been known for bullish behavior. He is often times very rude and condescending to members of the team. The team did not know that you all were related; however, after your promotion, Jim is overheard stating that "Yeah, the new team lead is my brother-in-law. I am going to get away with murder." How are you going to handle the situation?

Provide a detailed action plan to address the situation.

Activity – Who is more qualified?

The team lead position is open and you have decided to apply for the position. Sally, who has been a member of the team for five years, two years more than you, has also applied. You have more education than Sally and have come highly recommended by customers and the previous team lead due to your great personality and teamwork focus. After, a few weeks of interviews and follow-ups, you are offered the position. Sally is furious. Sally has spread rumors throughout the team that you must have gotten the position by having an inappropriate relationship with a "higher-up." Sally is not moving to another team and will remain a member of the team you now lead.

How are you going to handle the situation?

Provide a detailed action plan to address the situation.

CHAPTER SIX
Go Forth...and Lead

Go ahead and admit it, when you read the chapter title you thought about Charlton Heston in the Cecil B. DeMille film The Ten Commandments. I will admit when I wrote the title, I was thinking of Charlton Heston speaking from the mountain in the movie.

As you finish up this book, you are probably thinking, "there is much more to leadership, then I thought." Yes, there is. No one book, seminar, course, etc., can tell you everything about being a leader. It comes through trial and error. The key is not to be afraid to ask questions, listen to the ideas of others, be comfortable in your own skin, and have fun.

When in doubt, ask for help. Do not float around lost because you feel that as a leader you should know everything. Where is it written that leaders must know everything?

"Have fun?" Yes, leadership can be a lot of fun. It does not have to be a burden. You are in a position to help and motivate others, to listen to great ideas, work with great people. You want to have fun. If you see leadership as an albatross, you may not be in the right position for you. No position is worth your sanity.

Take the time to research your company and your team. Get to know both and understand the motivation for each area. Yes, the company as a whole has a motivation when it comes to employees and customers. Determine how your leadership style will complement the organization and your team.

As I stated in the first chapter of this book, I want my readers to understand who they are as leaders. You have to understand and work with who you are. Know who you are and build your foundation of leadership on this knowledge. It is okay to want to read books, go to leadership seminars, watch other leaders in action, etc. Through it all, ensure you are comfortable with being **you**. Now, go forth...and LEAD!

References

Merriam-Webster.com. (2017). Boss.
Retrieved from
https://www.merriam-
webster.com/dictionary/boss

Merriam-Webster.com. (2017).
Leadership. Retrieved from
https://www.merriam-
webster.com/dictionary/leadership

Thank you for purchasing my book.

If you have enjoyed the book, I would be grateful if you would post a review for it. If you have any questions, feel free to contact me at www.1drkris.com and I will respond as soon as possible.